In The Spirit of Adventure
A 1914 Smoky Mountain Hiking Journal
Written by D. R. Beeson

IN THE SPIRIT OF ADVENTURE
A HIKE IN THE GREAT SMOKY MOUNTAINS
August 28 - September 4, 1914

By

D. R. Beeson, Sr.

Edited By

Norma Myers

Ned Irwin

Charles W. Maynard

Panther Press SEYMOUR TENNESSEE

ISBN   0-9630682-7-X

Panther Press
P.O. Box 636
Seymour, Tennessee 37865
615-579-5230

This Work Is Dedicated To
D. R. Beeson, Sr.
And His Friend,
C. Hodge Mathes
Who Roamed the Mountains
In the Spirit of Adventure

The writer's royalty is being given to the Archives of Appalachia at East Tennessee State University and to Friends of Great Smoky Mountains National Park.

The Archives of Appalachia serve the region by preserving and providing access to records of historical and research value pertaining to the political, social, economic, and cultural development of the Southern Mountains. The original journal with other Beeson materials is in The Archives of Appalachia.

Friends of Great Smoky Mountains National Park is dedicated to providing support to Great Smoky Mountains National Park. The group is made of individuals, corporations and civic groups who give to fund projects within the Great Smoky Mountains.

For more information write:
Archives of Appalachia
Archives and Special Collections Of the Sherrod Library
East Tennessee State University
Box 70665
Johnson City, Tennessee 37614-0665

Friends of Great Smoky Mountains National Park
134 Court Street
Sevierville, Tennessee 37862

INTRODUCTION

August 30, 1994 8:00 P.M.
Spence Field

The sun sets in a blaze of glory. The perfect end to a wonderful day of hiking. We began our trek this afternoon on the Bote Mountain Trail, an old road from pre-Civil War days constructed with Cherokee help. The temperature has cooled considerably from the hot, humid climb. Now the stiff breeze chills us to the point of needing a jacket and wishing for long pants.

The rays of the setting sun catch the peak of Thunderhead where D.R. Beeson and Hodge Mathes camped exactly eighty years ago tonight. On that trip, intermittent showers dampened the two hikers but not their spirits on the first full day of their adventure across the crests of the Great Smoky Mountains.

Ours is an overnight hike to an Appalachian Trail shelter; theirs was a week long journey which took them from Kinzel Springs near Townsend to Big Creek on the Pigeon River. The packs we tote to the top are lightweights in comparison to Beeson's and Mathes' gear. Hodge Mathes, in writing for the Potomac Appalachian Trail Club in 1946, described their own equipment: "a `Compac' shelter tent weighing five pounds, blanket-rolls that proved too light for comfort in the September nights at those altitudes, small miner's lamps, and an extra flannel shirt apiece. The heaviest piece was Don's five-by-seven camera with film-packs and tripod. The rest was food, with canned pork-

and-beans as the chief staple, two bags of home-made, cracker-type biscuits (my wife's contribution), and a few dozen almond chocolate bars. As an emergency ration we took a bag of ground parched corn (the Cherokee `chickahominy'), which proved a godsend. And I must not forget my soul-comforting pipe and tins of tobacco. Don, poor fellow, doesn't smoke. Our two `rucksacks' at the start-off weighed close to 50 pounds each."

It's interesting to note that Beeson recalled the packs weighing only around 30 pounds. Maybe one estimate was at the base of the mountain while the other was at the top. I've noticed that an increase in altitude has an effect on the weight of my pack. Unlike Beeson and Mathes, we have traveled light, carrying only a little food and two sleeping bags. Chocolate is in our packs, too, and tastes good after the long climb.

A stone trail shelter will offer us protection from the fickle weather of the Smokies. Beeson and Mathes carried their own tent which provided only partial shelter from the elements. Their food wasn't the modern dehydrated or freeze dried fare we have, but was canned beans and cracker biscuits.

Their bulky camera with wooden tripod used 5" x 7" negatives. A fishing line provided a remote control so both men could be in some pictures. Their black and white images documented mountain scenery which looks very different through our 35mm camera lenses today.

The maps they used were so inadequate and inaccurate that being lost was a daily experience. Often their dead reckoning made them dead wrong about the trail's direction. They weren't in totally unknown territory, but it was poorly known. Today, maps and blazes and maintained trails patrolled by the park service afford us safe access to these wonderful mountains.

Change is inevitable, especially over a span of eighty years. In the failing light I notice rhododendron, blueberry, and mountain ash encroaching on the grassy bald where cattle freely ranged in years past. Even the mountains aren't constant but must endure some change.

The rugged mountains Beeson and Mathes traversed are now a part of the Great Smoky Mountains National Park, established twenty years after their hike. Early on many people, including Beeson and Mathes, urged protection of this special area. Now multitudes enjoy the Great Smoky Mountains National Park, which last year entertained over 9.3 million visits.

Eighty years ago the Little Tennessee River flowed freely through the valley below us. Fontana Lake now mirrors the fading blue of the sky. Fontana Dam wasn't built until World War II, thirty years after Beeson and Mathes looked down from these heights. In those days Cades Cove was a thriving farm community. Now cars crowd the well-known cove loop road carrying those who want to enjoy the beautiful mountain valley with its vistas and wildlife.

The Appalachian Trail presently covers the route recorded in this journal. I've enjoyed many stretches that Beeson and Mathes pioneered through Tennessee and North Carolina. They both supported the establishment of the long trail from Georgia to Maine in its early days. The white blazes that mark the route along the 2,100 mile length stand as memorials to the many who had the vision and determination to build a trail through these eastern mountains for all to enjoy.

Beeson and Mathes began their hike while the "Guns of August" were beginning to tear the world apart in Europe. The papers were full of the conflict when they returned from the tranquil trek. Today the news is of a possible U.S. invasion of Haiti. Sadly, some things have changed very little. Yet the mountains do provide a retreat from tensions and strife, if only for a moment.

Now that it is dark up on Spence Field, the late summer stars are out with a brilliance unparalleled in the valleys below. The stars have changed little in the past eighty years, but today's jets, planes, and satellites streak through the sky with speeds hardly imagined in 1914. Several meteors flash across the heavens tonight.

With David Morris, my friend and partner, I share conversation about hikes, families, adventures, hopes, and friendship. The first time I saw Spence Field and Thunderhead was with another friend, Hal Hubbs, on a twenty-three mile day hike from Clingmans Dome to Cades Cove (the reverse of Beeson's and Mathes' route). Spence has become a place of friendships for me.

Beeson and Mathes were friends as well as neighbors. They shared a love of the mountains and of hiking. These common bonds brought the architect and professor together on many occasions. The text of the journal is full of the enjoyment of two friends for each other and the mountains through which they walked.

On the next to last day of the Beeson and Mathes trip, they lost a German-made wide angle lens. The two didn't realize it until the next day when they were far down the trail. Two weeks later, they received a note from Walter Diehl of Knoxville. The lens had been found by Diehl, Dr. S.H. Essary, Franklin Bain, John E. Morgan and William M. Johnson. From this fortuitous discovery came a friendship between Diehl, Mathes and Beeson which blossomed to include Paul Fink and others.

Tonight those men seem close at hand as we hear the sounds of the barred owl on the next ridge and the wind through the tall grass, as we see the stars character the skies above Spence Field and Thunderhead, as we taste our hike supper, as we talk about everything and nothing. I'm glad this journal with its text and photographs is being published so that others can experience the sights and sounds, the playfulness and wonder, the hardship and friendship of C. Hodge Mathes and D. R. (Don) Beeson, Sr.

The two walked these heights eighty years ago as we walk today. In all that has changed I find the two men strangely familiar. Although I haven't had to labor under the difficulties they did, a part of me shares their motivation. For it was and is still done -- In The Spirit of Adventure.

Charles W. Maynard
Executive Director
Friends of Great Smoky Mountains National Park

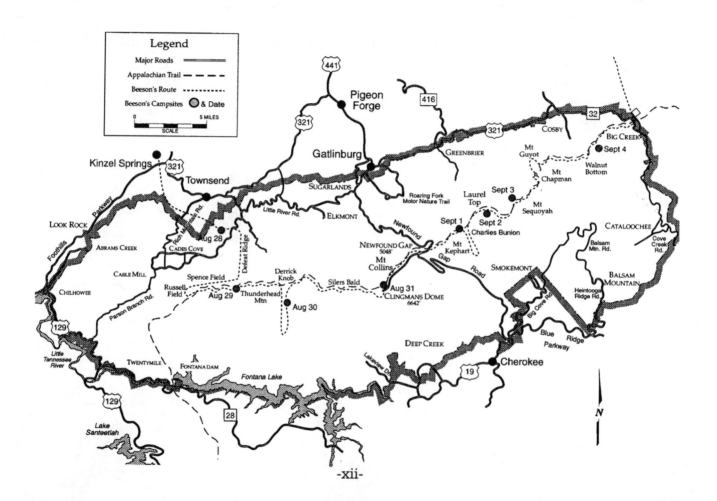

Hodge Mathes' Account of The Mileage For the Trip

August 29 - From the Dunn Place to the Spence Cabin	18 Miles
August 30-From Thunderhead to "somewhere in North Carolina"	16 Mi.
August 31-From "Blank Branch of Question Creek" to Clingmans Dome	17 Miles
Sept. 1 -From Clingmans Dome to a gap one mile east of Mt. Collins	8 Miles
Sept. 2 -On the Sawteeth Range, and Over Laurel Top	26 Miles
Sept. 3 -From Laurel Top to a nameless peak (probably Mt. Chapman) west of Mt. Guyot	10 Miles
Sept. 4 -From west of Mt. Chapman over Mt. Guyot and down to civilization	19 Miles
TOTAL for the Trip as Estimated By Hodge Mathes	113 Miles

These estimates appeared in an article by Hodge Mathes in the July 1946 issue of the Potomac Appalachian Trail Club Bulletin. It must be remembered that the estimates of distance are approximations and that the two often got lost which added many miles to their trek.

A NOTE ABOUT THE JOURNAL

The original journal which D.R. Beeson prepared now is in The Archives of Appalachia at East Tennessee State University in Johnson City. Many of D. R. Beeson's papers, journals, maps and photographs are held by The Archives of Appalachia.

Mr. Beeson actually kept a journal while on the trail. When he returned from the hike, he had his handwritten notes typed into a booklet which he illustrated with his photographs. This edition of his hike journal from 1914 attempts to preserve the look of the original. The text, photographs and captions are as Beeson wrote and arranged them. Only minor editing was done in order to make the text clearer and read more smoothly. Most of the photographs were prepared from the original negatives which members of the Beeson family located for this project. The map in this book was prepared from D.R. Beeson's own hand drawn route on a topographical map of the Great Smoky Mountains. Mr. Beeson drew his route on the map sometime in the 1940s, about thirty years after the hike.

The following is a representation of the original journal but not a facsimile. The editors and publisher attempted to preserve the character of the original while presenting an attractive book which can be kept and treasured as the actual journal is.

A WALKING AND CAMPING TRIP

THROUGH

THE GREAT SMOKY MOUNTAINS

It certainly looks like a bad start on a trip like this to sleep in a bed the first night out but we decided we are doing it to save time and get an earlier start in the morning,- and don't feel guilty at all.

Besides, these Dunns are old acquaintances of Mr. Mathes' and knew him when he taught at Maryville College some years ago. I think they have discussed most everyone that was ever connected with that institution.

The Deacon explained to them the hypodermic rattlesnake antidote, namely permanganate of potassium, which inserted under the periosteum in case of snake bite would immediately accentuate a counterirritant furinst the epidermis, thus creating, along with the accompanying spirits of frumenti, enough centrifugal inclination to antagonize the venomous influence of the venom. He showed them the apparatus and I guess they felt better about sleeping in the same house with it.

Looking East from Siler's Bald over Great Smoky Mountains.

The road from Riverside up Thunderhead Mountain.

The two of us, C. H. Mathes and D. R. Beeson, left Johnson City this morning on 41 and have had, so far, an uneventful trip. By continued questioning, we found that the best place to leave the railroad was Riverside which is a station in the foothills of the Great Smoky Mountains about thirty miles from Knoxville. The road runs up to Elkmont, a summer resort, mainly of Knoxville people, pretty close in to the base of the main ridge opposite Clingman's Dome which is one of the highest points on the range being given as 6619 by the state map and 6666 by a survey said to have been made when the Southern Railway built the Murphy Branch.

At the Riverside store, we got further directions from the storekeeper and as a result rode a lumber wagon 2^1/$_2$ miles and walked 1^1/$_2$ till we reached here. Mr. Sullivan, who drove the wagon, told us about a snake that is a new one on me and which I would like to see some specimens of. It is botanically known as the Joint Snake and has curious habits. He never saw but the one, tho he had always heard of them. He began beating it with a club when, much to his surprise, it began to

View in the Foothills of the Great Smokies.

fall apart at the joints like it was brittle. The most curious thing about the snake is that if you go away and leave it it will get together and grow back into one snake again. I'm not stretching this story a bit.

We have heard all sorts of bear stories and were warned at supper tonight against bear traps on top of the mountains. They are contrary to law but I guess law is scarce in the regions we are about to explore.

Last Sunday night, I talked with an old fellow at the Soldiers' Home in Johnson City, who used to be County Court Clerk at Sevierville, a small town some fifteen miles north of the big ridge. He gave me a lot of news about his region, warned me about the bear traps and told several very good bear stories to a large and appreciative audience. He was at Sevierville during the time of the reign of terror of the White Caps, organized just after the war as a protective measure against the depredations of a band of North Carolina outlaws who used to cross the Smoky Mountains, commit their crimes, and get back into the wilds across the border without any serious opposition from the ineffective protec-

The first meal on the way up Thunderhead.

tion of the law at that time. Hence the secret society of the White Caps was organized to take the law into its own hands and protect the regions along the Tennessee side of the mountains. The society seems to have served its purpose and freed the section from the raids from the other state, but, having no worthy cause to support and acting in strict secrecy, they turned their attention to doing some plundering themselves and eventually terrorized the community much more than the bands they organized to exterminate. Their reign is said to have lasted for a good many years and the fear in which they were held was so great that the citizens locked themselves in their houses at dark and closed the shades and never ventured out after nightfall. Driven to desperation, the good people in the larger towns finally sought the aid of the law, rose up in a body and, after convicting and hanging a few of the leaders, at last secured peace.

The house we are in tonight is the most pretentious we have seen in the country hereabouts so far and is very comfortably furnished. I am sitting in a near Chippendale mahogany chair as I make this entry.

"Our party" the first day out.

There is a "Balm of Gilead" tree in the front yard about which Mr. Dunn told us too late for us to get a good look at it tonight. The table before us is unusually good and the family about average mountain size, there having been sixteen children, nine boys and seven girls, with only one death and that after maturity.

Our camping outfit is the heaviest I have ever started out with and weighs about thirty pounds for each of us. We don't intend to break any speed limits, however, so I think we can manage.

Early Morning - Looking South from Thunderhead Mountain.

August 30, 1914, 6:00 A.M.
In camp on Thunderhead Mountain.

We are just breaking camp on Thunderhead at an altitude of about 5600 feet, after having slept wet,- in our clothes of course,- on account of having had to make camp in a hard rain last night about dark.

Yesterday initiated us pretty well into all the trials of mountaineering in all departments so that the future doesn't worry us any more than it did Omar Khayyam,- or does.

This mountain is about ten miles from the west end of the Great Smoky chain where the Little Tennessee breaks through, and is on the main ridge with an altitude slightly over 5600 feet. This morning is fine, the air is clear, our fire is a good one and the Doc is about due with the water he went to the cistern for a quarter of an hour ago. Then breakfast will occur.

The country for as many miles as you can see is decorated, and in many places, covered with the masses of white fog or cloud that rests

Early Morning - Looking Southwest from Thunderhead.

all over these mountains in the night time and fills up the valleys. To the south we can see the Nantahala Mountains some forty miles off and to the north, the same distance to the hills about Knoxville, all clear and beautiful.

Yesterday was a whole lot otherwise. It rained four times, not counting the showers, and consequently we were soaked four times good and plenty, clear in to the cerebellum and a few other times not quite so deep. We have quit wearing our hats and Mr. Mathes is using them for pads to keep the straps of his pack from rubbing his shoulders.

After we reached the top of the ridge soon after dinner we were in the clouds continually and in rain most of the time. The climb up was about 4000 feet in elevation in ten or twelve miles and good road all the way. We ate dinner at a famous cold spring near the top, then followed the road up to Spencer Cabin, an old landmark consisting of a herdmens' [cabin] a short distance down the North Carolina side of the ridge. The original cabin was on the Tennessee side and was burned by lightning and the second about a hundred yards distant shared the same fate not long ago.

Clingman's Dome from Thunderhead.

We lost about four miles of distance, some religion, and two hours time hunting these cabins and got in a hard-rainstorm in so doing. We met three herdsmen near the cabin who gave us some instructions about trails to Clingman's Dome. No person so far has been able, however, to give us any information on the region from there on to Guyot or what sort of country we may expect. The way to Clingmans seems pretty well known but from there on and after that the deluge may be our schedule. I hope we are not delayed enough to make our food supply run short for I don't believe even a food faster would care to tramp foodless over these mountains without anything to eat.

After the Spencer Cabin rain we had a dry and more enjoyable walk over to Thunderhead and it even brightened up enough to let me get a couple of pictures of the most unearthly view on record. Cade's Cove, ten miles to the west and four thousand feet below us, was covered with a mattress of clouds just high enough for the setting sun to sneak under on the far side and set the whole place on fire. It looked bad for the residents.

About then it began to rain again and we collected firewood and cut tent stakes in a driving storm which lasted about three quarters of an hour and quit just in time to allow us to start a shy backward fire and have supper in comparative comfort and superlative wetness. The sod we made camp on was like a wet sponge but the tent, with a sprinkling of balsam tips, for a mattress, stayed dry all night. The Deacon dried his self pretty well before turning in but I had such a time drying out the camera and films and the map that I retired as I was, drenched to the dew point. All present took the inconvenience in good humor, of course, and now it is all over for the time being, there are no resulting colds or stiffnesses present. It takes about fifteen minutes of good time, though, to pull on a pair of wet boots, so it's about as time saving to dry them the night before.

Looking Northeast from the ridge beyond Thunderhead.

August 30, 1914, 7:00 P.M.
Blank Branch of Question Creek,- i.e. LOST.

The day started very well as already outlined above and we got some
dandy views from the top of Thunderhead before starting on along the
ridge toward Clingman's, which is plainly visible or was till we got off
on the ridge and lost our way. LeConte also showed his lofty head to
perfection and is about the most prominent point we have seen so far.
He has about four warts on his head, the highest of which is about 6612
according to the United States Geological Survey. I scarcely think we
will have time to go out to LeConte, however, as the main peak is about
five or six miles from the main ridge we are trying to follow, which
would take up too much time. We have lost about a half day already today by being lost which will still further limit our time for future
exploration.

We reached the Hall Cabin, another herdsmen's gathering place like
the Spencer Cabin on Thunderhead, at 11:30 this morning and had dinner

The Hall Cabin.

at a fine spring a hundred feet or so from the top of the ridge. The
cabin is strongly built of logs on end and has a split shingle roof that
seems weatherproof. The window openings are closed with batten doors
fastened on the inside so we unwired the door and took a look in. The
chimney rises in the center of the room and three of the four sides are
taken up with built in bunks supplied with loose hay and a few straw
mattresses of the early Victorian period, and not cleaned since. The
table on the fourth side of the room seems to be used as a kitchen,
cooking being done in the open fireplace. The floor was puncheons and
serves as a protection for the food supply which can be had by lifting
the floor timbers and helping yourself. Our stock of beans and coffee
was still pretty good so we didn't investigate under the floor at all.
The cabin is used only when herdsmen are rounding up stock on the mountains and when they need some protection from the elements.

About half the length of the ridge we have been over so far has been
covered with thick soft grass like blue grass and little other vegeta-
tion except scattered scrub beeches.

Hall Cabin -
Inside.

We left the cabin at 12:50 and, with a good dinner on board, proceeded to celebrate by taking the wrong trail before we had gone more
than two blocks on our way. The Government map is so poor as to be almost useless till we get to Clingman's when we get onto another, and, I
hope, more accurate sheet of the Geological Survey. It is dated 1910
and should pretty well [be] fitted to the actual geography.

However, we turned south as the map seemed to me to advise and found
ourselves on such a good trail that we decided we had guessed right and
followed it about five miles toward the Gulf of Mexico, where we discovered a lumber railroad running up the valley so we started back to the
ridge by way of the railroad which must have come out at the lower end
on the Murphy Branch of the Southern. We kept with the railroad clear
to the head of the hollow and, darkness being imminent, camped here
without knowing for sure whether we were close to the main ridge or not,
I think we are within a mile or less of the top of the ridge, tho, and
should strike the trail some little closer to Clingman's than the point
where we strayed off. The getting lost was entirely my fault as I have

The Bull's Head
from near Hall
Cabin.

acted as guide from the start. The Deacon is not at all peevish on account of the mistake, so I don't suppose I am either.

The day has been clear of the fog that covered the mountain tops yesterday and we are hoping for a spell of good weather long enough to get us past Guyot and clear enough to keep the main points of the country in sight so as to give us our bearings.

Some animal with whose voice I am not familiar has been serenading us for the past half hour from up on one of the ridges but I hope he gets put to bed soon. It sounded a good deal like an elephant.

We are Fletcherizing on this trip and cutting down on the amount of grub we eat and have been hungry ever since we left the Dunn place. A real dinner would be fine scenery about now.

Near Hall Cabin -
Looking North.

August 31, 1914, 8:00 P.M.
Lost Again. Just over Clingman's.

Having got back to the ridge in an easy half hour of walking early this morning, we had got clear seeing and easy walking over Clingman's Dome, elevation 6666, and on a ways on the other side when the cloud settled down on us and we stopped seeing where we were going. Besides, the growth of all sorts was so thick as to give scarcely any view out and the ridge so wide as to make it well nigh impossible to tell where other ridges branched off at the sides. The brush began to get thick as we crossed the point and from there on two miles an hour was good walking. So we strolled about a mile down the wrong ridge before the compass showed us to be wrong. It was the toughest walking we have done yet and the briars and undergrowth so high that we couldn't see out at all. Fallen trees continually blocked the way and often took much engineering to get around, and added to that there was no trail for most of the distance, so we had to break our own. Here and there, an old survey line showed signs of having been cut out in bygone ages.

Clingman's Dome from Siler's Bald.

It was almost five when we got back to the main (we think) ridge so we tramped along it for a half hour or so and camped in a very wet place near a puddle of surface water that is new enough to supply our needs.

The first part of the day's trip, six miles to Siler's Bald, elevation 5500 feet, was about the best yet and enjoyed by all present. Water was plentiful as usual and the trail good and the prospect from Siler's immense. After that, the five miles to Clingman's was all up hill and the trail getting worse and worse. We reached the Dome about 2:30 after a feast of uncommon fine blackberries by the way which made up to a certain extent for the disappointment occasioned by not being able to see the surrounding country from this, the highest point in the Great Smokies. The mountain is very much flattened on top and densely wooded so that the sun light gets through in spots only and a person can't see out even in spots. So we didn't even stop at the top but kept on over and down this side.

From Siler's this morning we got our first good view of Guyot, 6636, about thirty miles or more away.

Herdsmen's Shelter near Siler's.

The immense scale of all this scenery up here causes you to want to look at it by the hour in silence. The great expanse is ahead of all I have seen heretofore. The ridges are the sharpest I have ever walked over but there are none of the imposing rock formations that are to be seen on Roan and Grandfather Mountains and Jonas Ridge. Everything else is on a very much greater scale.

The Woods on Clingman's Dome.

Big Balsam on
Clingman's Dome.

In Camp just beyond Clingman's Dome.

Tuesday, September 1, 1914, 7:30 P.M.
In a Gap, 5400 Feet, One Mile East of Mt. Collins.

I am glad to be able to say at last that we know where we are camping and that, while we were lost for an hour this afternoon, we are now located for sure and have made a fine dry little camp under some beech trees that grow so close together that the moonlight can't get through. The wind howls through the gap with a mighty lonesome sound. I wish we could stay awake longer so as to appreciate the moonlight more.

To the south, the heads of the valleys drop off with about the same slope as the steep side of Buffalo Mountain on the White Rock side, but on the north they fall straight down almost for about 3500 feet. They're too steep for a goat to stand on. As you can imagine, it gives rise to a wonderful outlook.

We made the first six miles today from camp to Indian Gap in good time notwithstanding the fact that we had to break our own trail a good part of the way through blackberry thickets ten feet high saturated to the dew point. Part of the time we ate our way through.

Natives Camping in Indian Gap.

We saw our first bear tracks this morning near Indian Gap. They looked too big for a bear but a couple of hunters we saw later at the gap where they were camped said it was just an uncommonly big bear. They had seen the same tracks, and assured us as usual that we were in no danger, which we have believed all along.

One of them told us a story about having taken a short cut over Miry Ridge one evening, armed with nothing but a fishing rod, when he ran across an old she bear playing with her two cubs. He stopped to watch for a minute but the old bear got wind of him and chased him along the ridge till they came to a log where he took a stand and frightened her off by shouting and waving his hat. This may be a good story to remember.

We visited at the Gap for a while but were not asked to dinner so went on out about a mile and ate as usual. From there on to Mount Collins, elevation about 6500, the way was the roughest yet and the ridge in most places just wide enough to support the granite boulders we crawled over. In fact it would have been no trouble at all to step off and down a couple of thousand feet on the right into North Carolina or the same on the left into Tennessee. To add to the difficulty, every-

LeConte (The Bull's Head) from Indian Gap.

thing was so grown up with briars that the footing was very hard to see.

About the middle of the afternoon, we passed the ridge that leads off to the north to the ridge called the Bull's Head Group, the chief point of which, LeConte, has an elevation of 6612 and supports a Government triangulation station. We wanted very much to go over but it was about five miles and we felt that we could not spare the time.

An hour later, we crossed Mt. Collins and were rewarded by one of the greatest views yet, especially to the north where it is especially high, deep, precipitous and boundless.

There is a state road [which] crosses the State Line and the main ridge at Indian Gap and it is the only cross trail we have happened on so far. It was built for a wagon road but could scarcely be used for such now without a lot of cutting away of fallen trees.

The deacon is about to retire and I must stop. The weather has been fine all day, the mists clearing about the middle of the morning and no rain at all.

State Road crossing State Line at Indian Gap.

All signs were encouraging when we arose as usual about 4:30 this morning. The sky was clear and the view overtaxed my descriptive powers to the usual limit. It begins to look like our digestive powers would be undertaxed, however, as it will probably take us till Friday night to reach the Pigeon River Gap which we counted on making by tonight. A ten ounce can of beans divided by two, a cup of coffee and three biscuits about as big as oyster crackers doesn't make a voluminous breakfast. We cut out the beans at dinner today and divided the last can of salmon,- a very small affair. Our suppers for the past three nights and for the future are consisting of a couple of handfulls of ground parched corn and a pint of water with a chocolate almond bar for dessert. We are both agreed that chocolate is a necessity on such trips as these. The blackberries have been a great help to us as a filler in and we hope they continue to line our paths. They are also a preventive of thirst.

*Looking North from
Mt. Collins.*

Just for a change,- we got lost before dinner today instead of after as is our usual custom. The time loss was about three hours and the trails all pretty rough, and we didn't reach Porters Gap till about one o'clock and without water.   So the first thing was a trip down straight about a thousand feet to lay in a supply.

A poor trail crosses the main ridge at this point and is marked by an old broken tombstone with a lot of additional initials cut thereon. The Gap is the lowest point between Clingman's and Guyot and has an elevation of about 5300 feet above sea level.

From the Gap on, we made about a mile an hour and I'm free to confess that I doubt if we could have this last part of our trip at all if the trail had not been broken to some extent quite recently by a party of two, from the footprints, a man and a boy. As it is, we do well to make over the mile an hour as extreme care has to be used on account of the narrowness of the ridge and the uncertainty of the footing. A slip to either side would generally mean serious consequences. The indications are that not very many people have ever made the last half of this trip.

Looking South from Mt. Collins.

There are places where you have to climb up or down the ends of boulders ten or twelve feet high or walk a fallen tree across a hole whose depth you can only guess at on account of the thickness of the undergrowth which hides the face of the earth completely.

In making camp tonight we have had to build up a flat area for our tent out of stones and branches and dirt, covered with balsam twigs to the thickness of about a foot. We are down from the crest of the ridge at the base of a cliff, having walked the last mile along the ridge, looking in vain for a flat space wide enough,- seven feet, - to pitch our tent on.

These moonlight nights in camp are pretty lonesome luxuries and have inspired my Partner to the extent of six quatrains of verse, which he has just read to me. I ought to be sure of good sleep.

Looking North from "Blowing Rock."

Thursday, September 3, 1914, 7:00 P.M.
On Second Peak west of Mt. Guyot.

Today will be able to stand alone as to our record day, so to speak,
namely, the day on which we have never lost our way,- so far as we know.
Of course there may be things not given to us to know as yet. Anyway
I've never noticed much difference in the satisfaction of being sure
you're right, no matter whether you are or not.

Camp was left at 6:30 this morning and the same hard, rough trail
resumed on a nearly empty stomach. About noon we saw signs of cattle
and dropped down the side of the ridge a short distance and found the
usual clear, cold spring with faint cattle trails leading off in several
directions. In going back up one of these we ran across a small shelter
about six feet square that looked too much like a moonshine still to
draw us into an examination. So we sneaked past and on reaching the top
of the ridge found a soap box with two one gallon jugs inside, behind a
big balsam. Didn't it look suspicious?

Looking Northeast
from "Blowing Rock."

Dinner was even lighter than yesterday and would have been scarcely worth mention unless we had had the old reliable blackberries to constitute the bulk of it.

All morning we followed a sort of a trail which we hoped would last till we reached Guyot but it stopped at the jug tree and we have been breaking our own trail since. Our day's distance today was about six miles so no records for speed are in danger. It reminds me of Mr. Mathes starting for Sunday School of a Sunday morning. However, we still hope to reach Guyot about noon to-morrow and camp beyond if we get stopped on the down grade, tho we will probably have to spend the day where we are if the clouds should shut in the mountain tops; there are several crooked ridges leading off about here and it would scarcely be safe to trust to map and compass alone. This stupendous mountain scenery has, nevertheless, repaid us for all our hard tramping and the memory of it will always be a source of pleasure to me. It's a blessing that such a recollection stays with a man so much longer than the memory of rubbed feet and half rations.

Laurel Thicket near Porter's Gap.

About the middle of the afternoon we discovered a new "Blowing Rock" that certainly makes the original in North Carolina act like a poor imitation. The flue that caused the draft and headed at the top of the ridge where we stood was about 1500 feet deep and almost sheer down to the head of a pretty green Tennessee valley. There is always some draft up the heads of these steep hollows and valleys but the direction of the prevailing winds must have some effect to cause such a pronounced draft in some certain places.

At any rate when the Deacon was cutting out brush and small branches for some pictures at this place not one piece would drop over into the abyss but all came right back to his feet and some were by no means light. We did not try to with a hat as my Partner has lost both his and mine.

We have put a call for 3:30 in the morning so I guess I will subscribe myself, Yours Truly, and turn in. This is the greatest trip yet.

A Beech Tree near Porter's Gap.

Friday, September 4, 1914, 9 P.M.
Crestmont, N. C.

All over,- except a hundred miles or so by rail. The scheme of making that early start this morning worked to perfection and, tho it was
the coldest night yet, we managed to separate ourselves from our tent at
3:30 and have our near-breakfast over by the time the sun appeared on
the scene about ten minutes of five. Hence we gained the summit of Mt.
Guyot, elevation 6636, at ten o'clock A.M. after a strenuous pull of 500
feet over Execution Ridge, then down about the same to Respite Gap and
up an unbroken ascent of over a thousand feet vertically to the summit
of Guyot, the most dismal spot on earth, I'm sure. It was, in a way,
the objective point of the trip, too, so we were a good deal disap-
pointed to be so sold. It seems like one of the highest points East of
the Mississippi, corner for about three counties in North Carolina and
five or six in Tennessee, a marker of the State Line and a peak scarcely
known at all to explorers,- it certainly seems like such a prominent

Mt. Guyot from Southwest.

feature ought to furnish some attraction when arrived at. But we looked all over it for about an hour and did not find a bit.

The mountain is so densely wooded, covered with small balsams about four feet apart, that you can't see out over the surrounding region except in a very unsatisfactory way at one place on the west side. To the East you can't see out at all. Half the trees are dead and the ground covered with thick, moist, green moss that squirts at you when you step on it. You can get lonesome there on a bright day with all your friends and a brass band. So we didn't stay long.

The morning's walking was the hardest of the trip. I was tired for the first time, and really attribute it to the lack of stuff to eat. Then the thickets were the worst yet,- almost jungles,- and more bear tracks to boot. The blackberries continued good and saved the day again as we were reduced to a can of beans, eight biscuits and two bars of chocolate for the day.

Well, after eating dinner (?) on Guyot we struck a bearing to bring us out on the head of Big Creek, and slid straight down the mountain 4000 feet lying flat so as to slide under the limbs of the "Laurel

On summit of Mt. Guyot, El. 6636.

Hells" as the thickets are called. Near the end of the slide we struck
a stream bed on a very steep angle,- no water at all but the smoothest
and soapiest soapstone I ever saw. It was pretty dangerous sliding and
we had to go slowly.

    At last, about 2:30 P.M. after being called safe on the long slide we
came out on the head of the Big Creek all right and struck a lumber operation employing about a hundred men whose manager took pity on us and
gave us a note of instructions to the head cook at the mess house, a
beautiful structure of rough boards and tar paper. At any rate, it had
all the requisites to beauty we could see. We were set down on a couple
of soap boxes and didn't have long to wait,- the four cooks were pleasant young white fellows,- well they let us begin; and I will never for-
get how good it tasted. I was sort of ashamed of both of us but we certainly did go through the field from Oysterlitz to the final assault on
Limberg and Custard's Last Stand. To cap the climax they refused to
charge us for the meal. The camp was about twelve miles above Crestmont,
six of whom we covered on a log engine and six on foot. So we ate another meal after we got here about dark. The cross ties seemed very

On the trail down from Mt. Guyot.

hard walking. We are at present in our suite at the Crestmont Inn and the Deacon has discovered that we have no wash water. We have done without any serious washing for eight days, tho, so you will no doubt say, "What's the use". I agree. We expect to reach Johnson City to-morrow noon.

Of course this has been the greatest of my walking trips and I won't know where to go next. I will always be glad to have travelled this range while it is still so unknown and untrod as it is now. The scarcity of provisions added zest and the element of uncertainty.

The weather has been mostly all in our favor or we could never had succeeded in making the trip at all. Both of us are a little thinner and considerably engrossed in uncut whiskers but are feeling fine and in good shape for a winter's work and play. Here's hoping we get another such trip next summer.

We are practically in the Pigeon River Gap on the North Carolina side, and the balance of the trip will be by rail so can be dispensed with.

- FINIS -

Waterfall - Head of
Big Creek, N.C.

Big Creek at Sunset.

Big Creek Lumber Co. Skiddder pulling logs from head of hollow
7000 feet away.

Pigeon River Gap. "White Rock," Eastern end of Great Smoky Mountains, in background.

Rainbow Falls - 1920s
D.R. Beeson's brother-in-law, Raymond Rankin, is to the right of the falls. Mr. Rankin was a Presbyterian minister and president of Tusculum College.

BIOGRAPHY

In the spirit of adventure, D.R. (Donald Richard) Beeson, Sr. moved to West Virginia to explore what to him was described as a yet untamed frontier. Beeson joined a tide of professionals who migrated to the Appalachians around the turn of the century as a part of the increasing industrial development of the region. His work with United States Steel in the coal fields and with the Clinchfield Railroad certainly would be worthy of study within the context of the economic history of southern Appalachia, but it is his love of the outdoors that makes his story special.

Beeson was born in 1881 in Uniontown, Pennsylvania. He was the youngest of three children in one of the leading families of Uniontown. His father, William Beeson, educated at Yale and Harvard, was an attorney and businessman. When D.R. Beeson, Sr. was seven, his mother Mary Conn Beeson died of tuberculosis. His mother's sister, Rebecca Conn, took over the responsibility for his care. The family maintained a residence in Uniontown so the children could attend school there, but Beeson spent his early years at Mount Braddock, a 1,500 acre family estate located six miles from Uniontown. Beeson remembered his childhood at Mount Braddock as a happy time, in summer hiking into the mountains to camp or swim, and in winter skating on the ponds or "coasting down the hills." In a reminiscence of his early life, Beeson recalled that he "ran wild" over the estate and "knew every stream and woods."

In 1888, his father's business failed, and in the economic depression of the 1890s, the family's wealth was lost. The family sold the Mount Braddock estate in 1891 and lived in Uniontown the year round. At age 10, Beeson began working as a newspaper boy where, as he described it, he learned the "survival of the fittest." After graduating from high school, he worked pitching hay on a farm. Beeson left Uniontown in 1898 to live with his aunt, Louisa Hamilton, in Washington, Pennsylvania. He attended Washington and Jefferson College, where he studied mathematics. Lacking the funds to continue his education, Beeson was forced to quit college at the end of his sophomore year.

In 1900, Beeson began working for the H.C. Frick Coal and Coke Company in western Pennsylvania. He earned thirty-five dollars the first month as a chainman for an underground engineering force in the coal mines near Connellsville. Within the next year, he moved to Scottdale to work as a draftsman in the company's main office. With the organization of U.S. Steel, the drafting department of H.C. Frick Coal and Coke Company was moved to Ambridge, Pennsylvania. By 1902, Beeson was working as a draftsman for the American Bridge Company, a subsidiary of U.S. Steel, which handled the steel construction operations for the new corporation.

In the spring of 1902, Beeson moved to Gary, West Virginia, as a part of the corporation's efforts to start a new coal operation on lands purchased in McDowell County. Beeson later related that "[m]ost all the boys in the Ambridge office wanted to get the call as we had heard plenty of wild tales about the region, and adventure seemed to have her hand out beckoning us to a mighty attractive possibility of new experience in a part of the USA that was pretty much untouched by the hand of what we considered as civilization." For the first year in Gary, Beeson and Frank Boes, a long time friend from New York state, lived in a tent pitched by a stone quarry until company housing could be constructed.

While living in Gary, Beeson began exploring the mountains around the coal camp on hikes with Boes. Both he and Boes had heard of the famous Hatfield-McCoy feud, and visited the area in 1903. Beeson wrote that stories of the feud were in the news from California to Maine and "were no doubt, considerably magnified by the time they reached our very receptive ears." Beeson described meeting one of the Hatfields in his account of this hike:

"A tall mountaineer appeared in the trail ahead, blocking our advance, so we pulled up for some talk. The stranger was a cadaverous looking guy but without the fierce, mean appearance we had been hoping to see. In fact he had a pleasant face tho the eyes were sharp and suspicious. He was dressed country fashion and carried a single-barrel shot gun. Our dreams of an ideal rough customer had faded . . . . It gave us a lift, of course, to learn that he was a Hatfield."

Beeson remained at Gary for about two years, during which time he and Boes made several hikes into the mountains. At Gary, Beeson developed an interest in photography and began taking his camera with him on his walking trips.

In 1905, the construction of the company plants in Gary was completed, and Beeson moved to Bristol, on the Tennessee and Virginia border, to work for George L. Carter, who was building the Clinchfield Railroad. After a couple of years, Beeson moved to Johnson City, Tennessee, when Carter moved his office there. Eventually, the Clinchfield expanded into the Carolina, Clinchfield, and Ohio Railroad, which extended its line from Spartanburg, South Carolina through the mountains to Elkhorn City, Kentucky. Beeson's work with the Clinchfield took him through the mountainous regions of North Carolina, Tennessee, Virginia, and Kentucky. Beeson struck out on his own in 1912 when he opened his architectural practice in Johnson City.

Beeson's interest in hiking did not end in West Virginia. In Johnson City, Beeson found a new hiking companion in C. Hodge Mathes, professor of English and dean at the East Tennessee State Normal School. On their first adventure together, Beeson and Mathes spent a week in September 1913 on a walking trip from Roan Mountain, Tennessee, across Grandfather Mountain to Blowing

Beech Mountain - 1929
(Left to right) - Mary, Betty (aged five years old), Dick, Mrs. Elma Beeson, Ann, Mr.
D.R. Beeson. The family walked to the top of Beech Mountain from Banner Elk, North
Carolina.

Rock, North Carolina. The two men first traveled on the Carolina, Clinchfield and Ohio Railroad from Johnson City to Tocane, North Carolina, then by foot to Roan Mountain. Beeson documented each part of the journey with photographs, and both men kept daily diaries during the trip. In his diary entry for September 1, Beeson described the early morning walk to the Roan High Bluff and the view from the northwest face: "...the big mountains in the distance stick up thru the morning fogs like islands. I could look at such a sight for a month. . . . However, I suppose I would come to regard it differently in time, tho the beauty could never die, - only the novelty would wear off." From the high bluff Beeson and Mathes traveled east to the High Knob near the Cloudland Hotel then followed the ridge at the Tennessee-North Carolina line to Grassy Ridge Bald, on toward Minneapolis, North Carolina and into Linville. On September 2, Beeson wrote they had gotten lost and it was his fault. He complained of passing through a grove of scrub beeches which was so thick they could not see out. They had to rely solely on the map and compass.

On Grandfather Mountain Beeson and Mathes found parts of the trail almost impassable "where a step of a couple of feet to the side would land you at the base of the cliff some five hundred feet below." Near one of the three peaks of Grandfather Mountain, Beeson and Mathes met another party of four, two girls and a man with "an extra civilized look" and a native guide. Beeson commented that probably he and Mathes did not appear very civilized to them. The two men were caught in a storm and were forced to spend the night in a cave on the mountain. Beeson noted that it was "worse to be on a mountain unable to get off than it is to be off when you can't get on."

Beeson and Mathes spent the next two nights at Findley S. Gragg's farm near the eastern base of Grandfather Mountain, with a day trip over to Blowing Rock. Leaving the Gragg's home on September 6, Beeson and Mathes walked to Banner Elk, North Carolina, near Beech Mountain, and

Dick, Betty and D. R. Beeson

then went to Elk Park on the East Tennessee and Western North Carolina Railroad. The total walking distance of their trip was calculated to be 127 miles.

Beeson and Mathes completed two walking trips through the mountains in 1914. On the first of the two hikes, Max Schoen and Buford Mathes accompanied them. The four men left Johnson City July 3 on the Carolina, Clinchfield, and Ohio Railroad and traveled through Erwin, Tennessee, and Spruce Pine, North Carolina, to the Linville Falls station. On the following day they began their hike along the Linville River to Table Rock and Hawksbill Mountains and back through the Linville River gorge to Linville Falls. Beeson commented that the "wildness of the region we are in makes the trip about the most satisfying I can imagine."

The four hikers made camp near Linville Falls on the last night of their adventure. The walking trip ended the following day at an inn near Pineola, North Carolina, where they caught the train home to Johnson City.

The twosome of Beeson and Mathes ventured on a second trip in the late summer of the same year. This trek took them along the ridges of the Smoky Mountain range on the Tennessee-North Carolina state line. In an article for the Potomac Appalachian Trail Club Bulletin, Mathes blamed Horace Kephart for their "rash decision to tackle the Smoky skyline." Both men had read Kephart's book, Our Southern Highlanders, and were discussing it during the summer of 1914. Beeson recalled the part where at Hall's Cabin, Kephart turned back a man who was intent on continuing to Mount Guyot. Mathes agreed that Kephart probably saved the man's life and mentioned that Kephart cautioned it would be difficult for experienced woodsmen with a "party of axemen" to make the journey to Mount Guyot. Beeson replied that it sounded like a dare to him, and the two began planning the trip for the coming fall.

LeConte Lodge atop Mt. LeConte - 1928
(Left to right) - T.C. Fry, Mrs. Elma Beeson, Ann Beeson(in background), Louise Fry,
Dick Beeson, Caroline Beeson Fry (D.R. Beeson's sister) and D. R. Beeson. Both
families made the hike to Mt. LeConte by way of the Alum Cave Trail.

On August 28, Beeson and Mathes took the Elkmont train from Knoxville to Riverside (now Kinzel Springs near Townsend) where they rode a lumber wagon for two and a half miles and walked another mile and a half to the home of Mathes' friend, W. H. Dunn, at the head of Dry Valley, Tennessee. The next day Beeson and Mathes walked south (18 miles in rain and fog) toward Thunderhead Mountain, near where they planned to spend the first night at a herdsmen's shelter known as the Spencer cabin. Beeson and Mathes proceeded east along the ridge of the Smokies, roughly where the Appalachian Trail is now located.

The two men reached Mount Guyot on September 4 after a week long hike on low rations over difficult terrain. From the summit the two men descended 4,000 feet, often sliding on their stomachs to pass under the "laurel hells." They eventually reached a lumber camp at Big Creek where they were fed. They spent the last night in the company inn at Crestmont, North Carolina, and rode the train home the next morning. Beeson described this hike as the greatest of his walking trips and wondered where he would go next.

The following year, Beeson and Mathes decided their next trip would be to the summit of Mount Mitchell. They began this journey on May 21 at Dolph Wilson's hotel in Murcheson, North Carolina. Beeson took pictures of the surrounding area, including a photograph of the old Tom Wilson cabin and of Dolph himself beside the skin of his 100th bear. Wilson agreed to guide the two men to the top of Mount Mitchell, and the three began the climb the following morning.

Wilson took Beeson and Mathes to Mitchell Falls where his father, Tom, had discovered the body of Dr. Mitchell, the mountain's namesake. From the falls the men climbed a ravine which Beeson described as having the "same slope as a telegraph pole" and when they found a place flat enough, stopped for lunch. Of Wilson, Beeson noted that he had "seen men before who could walk up a steep mountain as fast as he can but have never known one before who could talk incessantly while doing it." They reached the summit of Mt. Mitchell at 2:00 pm, but since the weather prevented good visibility, the three men went to the government weather station on the mountain. Wilson returned home, and Beeson and Mathes descended the east side of the mountain along a lumber skidway. Beeson commented that the east side was "bare and burned over and not a pleasant sight at all."

That evening Beeson and Mathes camped at the Blue Sea Fork of the Caney River which was just below the Pinnacle of the Blue Ridge. They hiked to the grassy knob of the Pinnacle the next morning. The two returned to Mt. Mitchell along a logging road. On May 24, they returned to Johnson City by way of the Carolina, Clinchfield, and Ohio Railroad. The hike to the top of Mt. Mitchell was the last of Beeson and Mathes' extended walking trips into the mountains.

Beeson's interest in hiking and camping became lifelong following his early excursions with Mathes. A religious man, he became equally faithful to hiking and attempted to convert others to this pastime whenever the chance arose.

His first attempt at a "conversion" came soon after the Great Smokies hike and concerned his wife, Elma Lillian Rankin Beeson. They met when Beeson, passing the open window of a church, heard her practicing a song. Elma Rankin was a music teacher in the original faculty of East Tennessee State Normal School (forerunner of East Tennessee State University) in Johnson City. The Beesons married in 1915, the year following the Great Smokies hike.

In August 1917, still early in their marriage, Don Beeson talked his wife into a week's hike in the Linville, North Carolina area. He called it a "co-ed" camping trip, and from the start it had some differences from his usual outings. As he noted in an unpublished account, "the eatables were a little above my usual grade and the gear included soap and towels for dishwashing,- a luxury peculiar to this one trip." Mrs. Beeson wore "high shoes" laced up a few inches above the ankle, as was the custom for women then, according to Beeson. He himself wore his usual hiking attire-- 16-inch leather hiking boots, trousers, a light shirt and a necktie.

The hike was remembered especially by Beeson (and his musical wife) for their visit with the McRae family, owners of Grandfather Mountain. The family was famous in the region for their bagpipe playing. "There were three of them at the time and they tuned up and gave us a short number as we paused on our way. It was some music; possibly it's a blessing that bagpipers are so scarce."

The later part of the journey was also well remembered. They were forced to work their way to the railroad junction against pouring rain and flooded streams. Finally, they reached the Linville Falls station, "soaked to the skin." Mrs. Beeson had to be dried out behind the stove of a country store and was only half dried when they boarded the train for Johnson City. With dry understatement, Beeson notes that "it is the only co-ed camping trip of my experience."

Beeson would later make a hike along this same line as escort to a party of industrialists from Kingsport who wanted to see some mountain scenery. He recalled the hard time he had getting the men (who were not in hiking shape) up to the mountain top. "At one time one of the men sat down on a rock and refused to go a step further, saying,- 'Here's where I get the effects of a Misspent life.'" This might serve as the motto of many a well-meaning, ill-prepared hiker.

If the attempts to make hikers of his wife or the industrialists were not so successful, Beeson found more success with his children--D. R. "Dick" Beeson, Jr., Mary Beeson Ellison, Anna Beeson

Troop 8
D. R. Beeson's boys.

Gouge, and Betty Beeson Helms, whom he often took on outdoor excursions. Don Beeson also found long-term satisfaction in his involvement with the Boy Scouts of Johnson City Troop 8, sponsored by Calvary Presbyterian Church of which he was a member. Through these efforts he exposed another generation to the pleasures of hiking the wilderness.

In 1920 Beeson agreed to serve as temporary scoutmaster of Troop 8 until a permanent replacement could be found. The temporary appointment lasted for the next twenty years. Troop 8 gathered its membership from the "poorer" part of town. For Beeson it was an opportunity "for getting the boys in contact with religious and spiritual matters," a side of their natures which might otherwise have been equally "underprivileged." A short devotional and prayer circle was a part of each scout meeting. Beeson also introduced twice a month hikes as a part of the regular routine. One was a day hike and one an overnight hike. In addition, a week long hiking/camping trip was held once a year. All this helped give the boys positive activities which kept them off the streets.

Over time Beeson developed a strong bond with his "boys." An architect by profession, he even designed and helped build a meeting house. Competition actually grew to gain admittance to the troop, as Beeson limited it to 32 boys at any one time. He was never easy on the troop, insisting that the boys earn anything they received. As would be noted in letters to him in later life, such lessons served the scouts well in adulthood.

The hikes were always vigorous, well planned, and often served to reinforce learning the boys received in school. One such hike was the attempt to locate the "Brown Mountain Lights" by survey triangulation. On this outing in the late 1920s, the troop divided into two groups, each with engineer's transits, one gang on Grandfather Mountain and one on Jonas Ridge. The groups

The A.B.F.M. Hiking Club
Paul Fink - Hodge Mathes - D.R. Beeson - Roy Ozmer
Cold Spring Mt. Spring 1925

sighted each other just before dark to get a baseline, with the idea of turning on the transit's lights after it got dark. It was a thoughtful plan, failing only to take into consideration the weather. "The night was unusually clear and none of us had ever seen the lights except when there was some haze in the air. So we came home next day without completing our triangle."

Such excursions only increased the popularity of the troop and of hiking among the troopers. Beeson gave up active work as scoutmaster just before America's entry into World War II. However, he kept contact throughout the war with many of his former scouts who served in far flung outposts of the world. The conditioning of the hikes and the lessons on woodcraft and life learned under Beeson, no doubt, made all of them better soldiers when duty called.

Beeson had always taken an active interest in his scouts' lives, not just in that part which touched on scouting. As one of "Beeson's boys" would recall "he was well known at the junior and senior high schools because of his habit of visiting these schools to check on his boys' conduct and progress...He went even further with several of his boys and advanced them sufficient money for their college education...Today there are architects, engineers, draftsmen, contractors, and other business men who owe their success to [him]."

Before, during, and after his scoutmaster career, Beeson remained an active hiker. As his architectural firm took more of his time, he had less time for extended hikes. A small hiking club was formed in 1930 around weekend hikes. It's members were Beeson, Hodge Mathes, Paul Fink (Jonesborough historian and naturalist), and local forest ranger Roy Ozmer (later known as "The Hermit of the Everglades"). They called their club "A. B. F. M. (Able bodied and Feeble minded)." Even after this "club" folded under family and business responsibilities, Beeson continued fulfilling what must have been a "need" to hike, to be away from the press of the city whenever the chance allowed. He had the habit of leaving the office soon after lunch on Saturday, driving to the base of Buffalo Mountain (on the southern edge of Johnson City), and hiking to the summit (a distance of about two miles) and back. It was on such a hike in the late 1940s that Beeson's active hiking career came nearly to a disastrous end.

He had made it about a half mile along the trail when he passed "a slim, cadaverous mountaineer going the same direction and carrying a single barrel shotgun." Beeson passed him and had gone on about 50 feet when he "heard a subdued crack from behind and felt a jar" on the back of his head. When "I felt the back of my head to investigate the damage, my hand came back covered with blood." Unsure of how seriously he might be wounded, Beeson feared going back down the trail to his car, since he would have to pass the place where the shot had originated. However, his fear of bleeding to death overcame this latter fear, and he hurried back. "My hair stood up on end and my knees got weak and sweat ran down my back along with the blood...It didn't occur to me until afterwards that he had only one barrel to his gun." Beeson made it to the hospital safely, the wound actually being slight. The doctor removed four of seven shot, deciding "the other three ought to stay as a souvenir of the occasion,- they are still there." Beeson's family, believing him to have encountered a moonshiner, refused him permission to hike Buffalo anymore. This did not deter him, however. He began driving some 10 miles further into Unicoi County to hike "the Pinnacle" there, and this remained his regular route for at least the next twenty years. In fact, he walked some six miles a day well into his eighties.

Beeson's love of hiking remained with him even after he could no longer actively engage in such extended journeys. He still made a determined effort to walk somewhere every day. Six years before his death in 1983, on his 96th birthday he wrote of his daily walk "to the Drug Store or Bank and back," a distance of about three blocks from the home he had designed years earlier, unaware that it would become base camp for this last "trail."

Norma Myers, Head of The Archives of Appalachia
Ned Irwin, Public Services Archivist

ENDNOTES

1. Beeson, D. R., Sr., "Autobiography," D.R. Beeson, Sr. Papers, Archives of Appalachia, East Tennessee State University, pp. 1-11.
2. Beeson, D. R., Sr., "Autobiography," pp. 2-11.
3. Reminiscences, D. R. Beeson, Sr. Papers, Archives of Appalachia, East Tennessee State University.
4. Reminiscences, D. R. Beeson, Sr. Papers, Archives of Appalachia, East Tennessee State University.
5. Beeson, D. R., Sr., "D. R. Beeson Itinerary-Uniontown to Johnson City," D. R. Beeson, Sr. Papers, Archives of Appalachia, East Tennessee State University.
6. Beeson, D. R., Sr., "Walking Trip, Grandfather Mountain," D. R. Beeson, Sr. Papers, p. 3.
7. Beeson, D. R., Sr., "Walking Trip, Grandfather Mountain," p. 5.
8. Beeson, D. R., Sr., "Walking Trip, Grandfather Mountain," pp. 9-13.
9. Beeson, D. R., Sr., "Walking Trip, Grandfather Mountain," pp. 19-20.
10. Beeson, D. R., Sr., "Walking Trip, Table Rock Mountain," D. R. Beeson, Sr. Papers, Archives of Appalachia, East Tennessee State University, pp. 1-4.
11. Mathes, Hodge. "A Week Among the Bears and Owls," Potomac Appalachian Trail Club Bulletin (July 1946) 65.
12. Mathes, "A Week among the Bears and Owls," p. 6; Beeson, D. R., Sr., "Walking Trip, Great Smoky Mountains," D. R. Beeson, Sr. Papers, Archives of Appalachia, East Tennessee State University, pp. 1-9.
13. Beeson, D. R., Sr., "Walking Trip, Great Smoky Mountains," pp. 29-33.

14. Beeson, D. R., Sr., "Walking Trip, Mt. Mitchell, N.C.," D. R. Beeson, Sr. Papers, Archives of Appalachia, East Tennessee State University, pp. 1-4.

15. Beeson, D. R., Sr., "Walking Trip, Mt. Mitchell," pp. 7-8.

16. Beeson, D. R., Sr., "Walking Trip, Mt. Mitchell," pp. 9-11.

17. Beeson, D. R., Sr., "Walking Trip, Mt. Mitchell," pp. 14-18.

18. D. R. Beeson, Sr. obituary, Johnson City Press-Chronicle, January 17, 1983, p. 2.

19. Beeson, D. R., Sr. "A Co-Ed Camping Trip, August 1917." D. R. Beeson, Sr. Papers, Archives of Appalachia, East Tennessee State University, p. 1.

20. Beeson, D. R., Sr., "A Co-Ed Camping Trip," p. 1.

21. Beeson, D. R., Sr., "A Co-Ed Camping Trip," p. 2.

22. Beeson, D. R., Sr., "A Co-Ed Camping Trip," p. 1.

23. Beeson, D. R., Sr., "A Co-Ed Camping Trip," p. 2-3.

24. Beeson, D. R., Sr. "Troop 8 History." D. R. Beeson, Sr. Papers, Archives of Appalachia, East Tennessee State University, p. 1.

25. Beeson, D. R., Sr., "Troop 8 History," p. 4.

26. Huff, Raymond E. letter, Feb. 4, 1971. D. R. Beeson, Sr. Papers, Archives of Appalachia, East Tennessee State University.

27. Beeson, D. R., Sr. letter, August 10, 1974. D. R. Beeson, Sr. Papers, Archives of Appalachia, East Tennessee State University.

28. Beeson, D. R., Sr. "Moonshining." D. R. Beeson, Sr. Papers, Archives of Appalachia, East Tennessee State University, p. 1.

29. Beeson, D. R., Sr., "Moonshining," p. 1.

30. Beeson, D. R., Sr., "Moonshining," p. 1.

31. Beeson, D. R., Sr. letter, May 3, 1977. D. R. Beeson, Sr. Papers, Archives of Appalachia, East Tennessee State University.

GLOSSARY FOR BEESON JOURNAL

<u>41</u> - The designation of a southbound Southern Railroad train that passed through Johnson City then to Knoxville.

<u>Balm of Gilead Tree</u> - Balsam poplar (Populus balsamifera) is a northern hardwood which was used as an ornamental tree. A "balm" made from the resinous buds was used in home remedies.

<u>Big Creek</u> - A large creek in the eastern end of the Great Smoky Mountains National Park which flows from the flanks of Mt. Guyot. The area was heavily logged by the Crestmont Lumber Company during the time of the August 1914 hike. Evidence of the logging operations is still visible today.

<u>"Blowing Rock"</u> - No known references to a "blowing rock" can be found. It is possible Beeson is talking about the way the wind blows up around Eagle Rocks or the Sawteeth.

<u>Buffalo Mountain</u> - A mountain outside Johnson City, Tennessee which Beeson regularly hiked in his later years. Beeson was shot with buckshot on a hike up Buffalo Mountain in the 1940s. Not seriously wounded, he made his way back to Johnson City where some of the buckshot was removed. It was thought that the mountaineer had mistaken the neatly dressed hiker for a revenue agent.

<u>Bull's Head group</u> - The name for the group of peaks surrounding and including Mt. LeConte. The term came from the observation that the mountain looked like a bull's head. Bullshead is now the name of one peak southwest of Mt. LeConte.

<u>Cade's Cove</u> - A scenic mountain cove in which Cherokee lived and whites settled in the early 1800s. This beautiful area in the western end of Great Smoky Mountains National Park has some of the original settlers' cabins and buildings preserved today.

Clingman's Dome - Clingmans Dome is the highest peak in the Great Smoky Mountains National Park and along the entire 2,100 mile length of the Appalachian Trail at 6,643 feet above sea level. Today a lookout tower one half mile from the Forney Ridge Parking Area provides a 360 degree view over the tops of the dense spruce-fir forest. It was named for Gen. Thomas L. Clingman, a soldier, statesman and lover of the mountains, who climbed the peak in the early 1800s. Clingmans Dome was also known as Kuwahi or mulberry place by the Cherokee and Smoky Dome by early settlers.

Crestmont Inn - A hotel operated by the Champion Lumber Company at Crestmont.

Crestmont, North Carolina - A large logging operation run by the Champion Lumber Company was located on the banks of Big Creek near its confluence with the Pigeon River near the present Big Creek Campground. The mill was built around 1904. The logging operations had extended up Big Creek to the base of Mt. Guyot by 1914. Beeson and Mathes ran across some loggers with Champion on the upper reaches of Big Creek. They rode a log train to Walnut Bottoms. From there they walked down track six miles to Crestmont Inn where they stayed the night.

The Deacon - A reference to Hodge Mathes because Mathes, the son of a Presbyterian minister, was a deacon in the Presbyterian Church. Beeson also refers to Mathes as Doc and the Professor because of Mathes' teaching at East Tennessee State Teachers College (later East Tennessee State University).

Dry Valley, TN - The site of the Dunn home in which Beeson and Mathes lodged their first night. The valley is located south of Tuckaleechee Cove and in the shadow of Rich Mountain outside the present day boundaries of Great Smoky Mountains National Park.

The Dunn Place - The home of W. H. (William Hurst) Dunn was in Dry Valley below Schoolhouse Gap. Several of the sixteen Dunn children had been students of Mathes' at Maryville College. One son, Charles S. Dunn, became a ranger with the park service and later an assistant superintendent of Great Smoky Mountains National Park under Ross V. Eakin. Durwood Dunn, W.H.'s grandson and Charles' son, is the author of Cades Cove A Southern Appalachian Community published by The University of Tennessee Press.

Elkmont - A small "village" of summer cottages that lined the banks of the East Fork of the Little River. The Wonderland Hotel and numerous cabins were in the Elkmont area until 1993 when the park service closed the area. A train line ran from Knoxville through Townsend up the Little River to Elkmont. It was on this logging and tourist line that Beeson and Mathes rode.

Execution Ridge - A name given to the last steep climb just west of Mt. Guyot. This may be referring to Tri Corner Knob.

Fletcherizing - After the American dietician, Horace Fletcher (1849-1919), who advocated the practice of chewing food slowly and thoroughly as an aid to digestion. Beeson is making fun of their small amount of food saying that they had to chew it slowly since there was so little of it.

furinst - A mountain way of saying "against."

Guyot - Mt. Guyot, named after the famed geographer and explorer, Arnold Guyot, is the second highest peak in the Smokies at 6,621. Guyot made a comprehensive study of the Smokies in 1859, naming many peaks and features. The Appalachian Trail does not cross the summit but winds around the Tennessee slopes of this peak which straddles the state line on North Carolina and Tennessee.

Hall cabin - According to Hiram C. Wilburn "This location was on the Tennessee - North Carolina state line in a high, flat gap approximately 3 1/2 miles east of Thunderhead. It was built by the Calhouns and Halls of the Hazel Creek area about 1885 as a [cattle] ranger's cabin. It was used mainly by people living in the Hazel Creek area, but any one -- [cattle] rangers, hunters, hikers -- who passed that way took shelter under its roof." Beeson and Mathes looked the building over and left a record of their passing by writing on its walls, as was the custom. It was from this writing that another party led by Walter Diehl knew where to send the lost and found camera lens. Hall's Cabin was located on what is today called Derrick Knob.

Indian Gap - The gap through which a "state" road came over the Smokies. It is said that an Indian trail preceded the crude road that was built over the mountains. Today the Road Prong Trail follows the route of the old road from the Chimney Tops Parking Area to Indian Gap which is on the Clingmans Dome Road. Indian Gap is about 1 1/2 miles west of Newfound Gap.

Jonas Ridge - A prominent ridge near Grandfather Mountain that Beeson would later take his scout troop to on several occasions.

Laurel Top - This 5,865 foot peak is 7 1/2 miles north east of Newfound Gap on the Tennessee - North Carolina state line.

LeConte - Mt. LeConte at 6,593 feet above sea level is the third highest peak in the Great Smoky Mountains. Its four points are West Point, Cliff Top, High Top, and Myrtle Point. The Boulevard connects LeConte with the main crest of the Smokies near the summit of Mt. Kephart (or as Beeson called it, Mt. Collins). The whole mass was called The Bull Head Group by early settlers. The name Bullhead now refers only to the western most point. The Cherokee called the mountain Walasiyi which referred to a mythical green frog. The name LeConte is after Joseph LeConte, a famed geologist, who reportedly worked with Prof. S. B. Buckley in the 1850s to map the Smokies. LeConte Lodge was operated on the peaks of Mt. LeConte beginning in 1925. The Beesons stayed in it in the late 1920s. It is the only place of lodging within the bounds of Great Smoky Mountains National Park today.

Limberg - A jocular reference to limburger cheese and Limburg Germany.

Little Tennessee River - A main tributary of the Tennessee River that flows from northeastern Georgia by the western end of the Smokies into the Tennessee near Lenoir City.

Maryville College - Hodge Mathes taught at this Presbyterian college in Maryville, Tennessee from 1905 to 1911. Mathes was born in Maryville in 1874 and received his masters degree from Maryville College in 1904.

Miry Ridge - A ridge which runs from Blanket Mountain south to the crest of the Smokies at Cold Spring Knob.

Mount Collins - The peak Beeson refers to as Mt. Collins is today called Mt. Kephart after Horace Kephart. Beeson and Mathes "blamed" Kephart for their adventure. The 6,217 foot peak, located on the state line about 3 miles north east of Newfound Gap, was named after Kephart when the park was created. The designation of Mt. Collins was given to a peak 3 miles northeast of Clingmans Dome. The name is from Robert Collins, native of the area, who guided and assisted Arnold Guyot in his explorations in 1859.

Murphy Branch (of Southern Railway) - Southern Railway built a line into North Carolina by way of Murphy. Don Beeson was a draftsman on this project before he began his own business in Johnson City.

Nantahala Mountains - A range of mountains south of the Great Smoky Mountains near Bryson City, Sylva and Andrews.

Oysterlitz - A playful reference to eating and the Napoleonic battle at Austerlitz.

Pigeon River Gap - The point at which the Pigeon River crosses from North Carolina into Tennessee. This is near the present Waterville Exit on I-40.

Porters Gap - A gap on the Tennessee - North Carolina state line between the Porters Creek (TN) and

Bradley Fork (NC) drainages about 5 1/2 miles northeast of Newfound Gap. It is a high gap at 5,500 feet above sea level.

Respite Gap - A fanciful name given by Beeson to the gap just west of Mount Guyot. It is probably the gap at the junction of the Appalachian Trail and Balsam Mountain Trail which is where the Tri Corner Knob Appalachian Trail Shelter is located today. It was a respite between the two steep climbs.

Riverside - Now known as Kinzel Springs just north of Townsend. Riverside was a stop on the railway from Knoxville to Elkmont on the banks of the Little River.

Sevierville, TN - The seat of Sevier County located about fifteen miles north of the crest of the Smokies.

Siler's Bald - A grassy bald on the Tennessee and North Carolina state line in Sevier County, Tennessee and Swain County, North Carolina. It is 5,620 feet above sea level.

Spencer Cabin - According to Hiram C. Wilburn: "This location was 1 1/2 miles west of Thunderhead just on the Carolina side. It was built and used mainly by cattle rangers from the Cade's Cove area in Tennessee; but like Hall's Cabin it served as a shelter for many years for [cattle] rangers, hunters and hikers. It was in existence prior to 1881." It is more accurately named "Spence Cabin." The "r" somehow crept into pronunciation and spelling over the years. Beeson and Mathes spent time and miles looking for the cabin but never actually found it.

Thunderhead Mountain - At 5,527 feet above sea level Thunderhead Mountain derives its name from being up in the thunderheads of many summer storms. Beeson and Mathes certainly experienced the rain part of this mountain's name. Thunderhead is located on the Tennessee - North Carolina state line southeast of Cades Cove.

White Caps - A group in Sevier County that was formed around 1892 to "clean up the communities." This group of vigilantes eventually terrorized many people. Another group, the Blue Bills, loosely organized to oppose the White Caps. The reign of the White Caps came to an end around 1898 after the murder of a couple. The resulting trial, conviction and execution effectively ended the White Caps in Sevier County.

ACKNOWLEDGEMENTS

The assistance of D.R. Beeson's family is gratefully acknowledged. D.R. (Dick) Beeson, Jr. of Johnson City, Tennessee, Mary Rankin Beeson Ellison of Winter Park, Florida, Ann Campbell Beeson Gouge of Johnson City, Tennessee and Elma Elizabeth (Betty) Beeson Helms of Neenah, Wisconsin assisted through their memories of hikes with their father and mother as well as with cherished family photographs which they generously shared.

Also, thanks to Georgia Greer of The Archives of Appalachia, who transcribed the original journal and to Jean Speer, the Director of the Center for Appalachian Studies and Services for her support. East Tennessee State University is appreciated for its role in providing personnel and support in the valuable area of preserving and protecting Appalachian history.

The work at Panther Press could not take place without the diligent service and careful eyes of David and Lin Morris, Hal and Elizabeth Hubbs, and Janice Maynard. Their foresight in bringing this valuable journal to the light of publication is truly appreciated.